Woman

LIVING IN GRACE

Jane L. Fryar

Woman of God®
Living in Grace
by Jane L. Fryar

Copyright © 2007 CTA, Inc.
1625 Larkin Williams Rd.
Fenton, MO 63026-1205
www.CTAinc.com

PRINTED IN THAILAND

Introduction

Family. Friends. Neighbors. Co-workers.
While people can pose our biggest problems
and bring on our biggest headaches, people
also grace the moments of our lives, bringing
meaning and joy to our existence. How gray
and empty life would be without those
worrisome, wonderful relationships that
come to us as gifts of grace from our
heavenly Father's throne!

This book contains devotional readings, Bible
verses, poems, and promises all designed to
help you celebrate your relationships —
relationships with your Lord and with the
people whose lives touch yours day by day.

Each week's readings include one longer and
two shorter devotional thoughts drawn from
relationships described in Scripture. Tucked

in among these devotions you will find space in which to respond as you journal, create a poem or prayer, draw a diagram or picture, or attach a photo or other memento.

Woman of God, we hope you find the devotional thoughts presented in these pages to be meaningful. But even more, we hope you will personalize the ideas introduced here. As you do so, we pray that you will grow in your most important relationship — the relationship of grace that your Savior, Jesus, has established with you!

Grace and peace be multiplied unto you
through the knowledge of God,
and of Jesus our Lord.

2 Peter 1:2 KJV

Luke 18:15–17

The Family of God

BLESSED BY GRACE

A Touch of Grace

New parents and grandparents can't seem to take enough photos. The grainy ultrasound before the infant is even born. The photos of baby's first day. The first tooth. The first step. The first bath. Scrapbooks and photo albums fill up quickly.

Christian parents usually also include photos of baby's first visit to God's house, and most churches welcome newborns in ways worthy of remembering. Traditions and teachings vary, but nearly all churches welcome babies, in part, by blessing them.

Our Lord Jesus welcomed and blessed infants and children this way, too:

> *People brought babies to Jesus,*
> *hoping he might touch them.*
> *When the disciples saw it,*
> *they shooed them off.*
> *Jesus called them back.*
>
> *"Let these children alone. Don't get*
> *between them and me. These children*
> *are the kingdom's pride and joy."*
> *Luke 18:15–16* THE MESSAGE

What a picture of grace, a portrait of family! Can't you just see Jesus opening his arms wide to enfold a lap filled with toddlers? Can't you picture the twinkle in his eyes and hear the gentle blessing he speaks over each boy and girl?

In the pagan world of that time, children had little standing, but the God of Israel saw it differently. He reminded his people again and again that children are heaven's gift, God's reward (Psalm 127:3).

It's no accident that Scripture calls all believers—whatever our age—"children of God" (for example, 1 John 3:1–2). Yet we adults often have trouble picturing ourselves in this way. The complications and responsibilities of adult life may blind us to Jesus' open arms. We may miss the smile of joy with which he welcomes us every time we come. Every time!

We may even shrug off his gentle touch of blessing and his invitation to leave our cares and worries at his feet.

We need not! The one who carried our sins on his own shoulders to the cross now holds out his nail-scarred hands in welcome. He yearns to brush away our tired frown and wipe away our tears. He longs to speak quiet words of blessing into our lives.

Simple, childlike hope and faith can be yours right now. Just ask!

My Thoughts,
Prayers, Memories . . .

Use these pages—and the ones like them throughout this booklet—
to record your response to the thought starters we've provided.
You may want to write a poem, attach a photo, or journal
your ideas. However you choose to respond, do so from a
heart filled with joy in our Lord's amazing grace.

The "Kingdom's pride and joy"!

"Jesus called them back" (Luke 18:16 THE MESSAGE).
Jesus calls me back, too!

A snapshot of God's grace in my life:

The Simplicity of a Child

Moms care for infants simply because infants need care.
We care for little ones, providing food, comfort, and attention
in times of hunger, fear, or pain. Why? Not because we expect
children can repay us. Not because they have earned our help.
We attend to their needs simply because of the needs!

Jesus received and blessed babies not because those babies
had earned his love and attention but simply because they
needed his blessings, simply because their parents
brought them.

Simplicity. Childlikeness. Trust.

Jesus tells us that unless we come "like a little child," we will
not be able to receive his kingdom at all (Luke 18:17)!

Can it really be that easy? Yes. Don't we have to clear a few
hurdles, pay our dues, meet some
minimal prerequisites? No.

We simply bring
our need to Christ's
cross and there
receive his pardon
and limitless love.

Come! Simply come!

10

A Simple Invitation . . .

As I ponder Jesus' invitation to simply come, I . . .

Dear Jesus,

I'm hungry for . . .

Do you have a Band-Aid for . . .

Will you come with me to . . .

"Who Let You in Here?"

We half expect the angel Gabriel might say it! We half expect he might challenge our presence in our Lord's throne room in much the same way the disciples challenged the moms and dads, grandmas and aunts, friends and neighbors who brought the children to Jesus so he would bless them.

But that will never happen. And even if it would, we have an answer: Jesus Christ, God's Son, our Savior himself has invited us. On Calvary's cross he flung wide the doors of heaven's palace. He has not only invited, but urged and even commanded us to come! A command of grace!

We belong to the family of God, the household of faith. "Now we are children of God," John assures us, "and what we will be has not yet been made known. But we know that when [Jesus] appears, we shall be like him, for we shall see him as he is" (1 John 3:2).

To be with Jesus now, to know his tenderness, his embrace, his forgiveness, despite our sin—what a blessing! To be like Jesus forever, to know what it means to love even as we have been loved—what bliss!

Grant it, Lord Jesus!

The Blessing

In blessing the children, Jesus also blessed their families.
Jesus has blessed me by . . .

Count your many blessings;
Name them one by one,
And you will discover
What your God has done!

The LORD bless thee,
and keep thee:
The LORD make his face
shine upon thee,
and be gracious unto thee:
The LORD lift up his
countenance upon thee,
and give thee peace.

Numbers 6:24–26 KJV

Luke 10:38–42; John 11:1–44

Sisters Forever

UNITED BY GRACE

A Gracious Host

Bring out the best china. The linen napkins, too! And a thorough housecleaning. Wipe down every cobweb. Mop all the floors, and not with that silly stick mop, either! Get down on your knees so you can spot the spots that lie partially hidden beneath the cabinets. Oh, and the menu. Yes, the meal must be as special as our guest. Whatever shall we serve?

Martha's thoughts raced full throttle as soon as she heard Jesus was coming. We don't know if she sent a formal invitation or if the visit happened as one of those "I-just-found-myself-in-the-neighborhood" serendipities that brighten everyday life.

However it happened, Martha graciously welcomed the Lord into her home (Luke 10:38). The house did not belong to Brother Lazarus; it was Martha's. Single women commonly own homes in our day, but not in Martha's.

Something else sets Martha apart as uncommon: She brooks no nonsense. Plainspoken, when she catches Mary shirking, Martha confronts the problem. She takes her case to the Rabbi himself, her honored guest. And she leaves no doubt that she expects immediate justice (v. 40): "Lord, don't you care that my sister has left me to do the work by myself?"

Lord, don't you care . . . ? For Martha, to care is to act: to make the meal, mop the floor, buy the house for one's family members, confront the problem. In her zeal, Martha does not stop to think about what she's really said.

18

Jesus cares, cares indeed! But not about the work and who's doing it. Instead, he cares about Martha's anxiety, about the burden she has placed on herself under the guise of serving him.

Jesus wants nothing, absolutely nothing, to come between Martha and the relationship he was dying to establish (or to come between us and the relationship he *did* die to establish)!

It was Martha's house, but Jesus was the host. He had prepared a banquet of most tender grace. He served up a big slice to Mary and to Martha. Still now, today, he serves it.

Won't you come on in?

*My Thoughts,
Prayers, Memories . . .*

Use these pages to record your response to the thought starters
we've provided. You may want to write a poem, attach
a photo, or journal your ideas. However you choose
to respond, do so from a heart filled with
joy in our Lord's amazing grace.

If Jesus came to my house . . .

Jesus has come to my house!

Why Can't You Be More Like Your Sister?

Did you have a sister everyone adored? A diligent one?
A beautiful one? A person who could have made a living as a
professional comedian, given her gift for impersonations and
sending a whole room into gales of side-splitting laughter?

Mary may have heard it over and over: *Why can't you be more
like Martha?* Her house is immaculate! She's the world's
best cook! Why can't you be more like your sister?

Then Jesus' visit turned the comparison game
inside out. Mary heard it with her own ears:
Martha, Martha, come! Sit down. Relax.
Be more like your sister!

No condemnation, but certainly
an invitation, an invitation to
drink in the grace of God, to taste
the sweetness of a love better than
dessert, better than chocolate!

That invitation stands open still
today, open to every one of Martha's
sisters—and Mary's sisters, too.
Come! Relax in your Savior's presence.
Drink in the grace of God! Taste the
sweetness of his forgiving love!

What are you waiting for?

22

A not-so-pretty picture—
things that keep me from
feasting on God's sweet Word.

What I want to say to Jesus about that . . .

I long to be more like my big Brother,
Jesus. Lord, help me! Especially . . .

Sisters — Together!

Lazarus, the brother of Mary and Martha, fell ill. Gravely ill. When he did, Scripture tells us, "the sisters sent word to Jesus" (John 11:3). Note that plural.

Also note the fact that as Jesus spoke with each sister alone after he arrived four days later, each spoke exactly the same words: "Lord, if you had been here, my brother would not have died" (vv. 21, 32).

The sisters had been talking, sharing their grief. In times of crisis, they clung to one another, united in love.

When Jesus raised Lazarus, contrary to their boldest hope, Mary and Martha shared the joy. They threw a party. Martha served (of course!). Mary, impractical and impulsive (of course!), worshiped in another way—pouring out on Jesus' feet the perfume that probably represented her whole dowry (John 12:2–3).

The sisters' story ends here. Each honoring the other's choices, the other's strengths. Sisters—together. Sisters—forever.

Has our Lord ever given you this kind of bond with someone else? Reflect on that relationship now, and thank Jesus for it!

A Celebration of Sisters!

Sisters—Together—in Jesus!

Sisters Laughing:

Sisters Sharing:

Thank you, Jesus, for sisters—
by blood and by friendship . . .

Do you remember . . .

. . . that tea party you prepared for all your dollies when you were six or seven? Do it again!

But this time:

- Invite one or three or ten real sisters— sisters in your family or "sisters" in the faith.

- Clean like Martha—or at least until you can find the tea pot (and the stove)!

- Plan impractically like Mary—or at least impractically enough to ignore for one afternoon the calories in the crumpets or pralines.

- Make a centerpiece that proclaims "Sisters Together, Sisters Forever."

- Then welcome your guests and laugh together until tears stream down your cheeks and no one ever wants to leave.

- Thank Jesus for sisters and friendship.

Luke 1:39–45

Friendships That Last

CONNECTED BY GRACE

Friends in Crisis,
Friends in Joy

Six months pregnant, Elizabeth would never have believed it
had she not already felt the baby moving in her womb. *John.*
The baby already had a name, the name the angel had given to
Elizabeth's husband, the priest Zechariah, in the vision that left
him speechless.

Now Elizabeth knew how Sarah had felt, pregnant at 90!
As with Sarah, so with Elizabeth, age had all but ruled out
the possibility of bearing a child. Yet like Abraham, Zechariah
would know the joy of bouncing his own baby boy on his knees.

Then one morning yet another surprise. Down the road and up
the hill to Elizabeth and Zechariah's house came a teenaged
cousin — Mary. She ran, and as she approached, Elizabeth's baby
fairly danced within her. "Could this be normal?" The question
must have flitted through Elizabeth's mind.

At once the Holy Spirit made clear exactly what was happening.
Elizabeth burst out in prophetic utterance:

> *Blessed are you among women,*
> *and blessed is the child you will bear!*
> *But why am I so favored,*
> *that the mother of my Lord should come to me? . . .*
> *Blessed is she who has believed*
> *that what the Lord has said to her will be accomplished!*
> *Luke 1:42–45*

The two had a lot to talk about. One pregnant after menopause, the other pregnant without intercourse. If nothing else, God had a sense of humor! How these two women must have laughed — and cried. While everyone else in their villages and in their own family may have doubted their stories about angels and mysterious pregnancies, these cousins believed each other. How good it felt, how relieved they were, to know each other's support.

What had Gabriel told Mary? "Nothing is impossible with God" (Luke 1:37). Here they sat — Elizabeth and Mary — living proof of *that!* Friends in faith.

Has God given you a friend like that? A friend to whom you can pour out your heart? A friend to whom you can confess your fears, your hurts, your sins? A friend who shares your joys, who assures you of forgiveness in the cross and the open tomb of Mary's Son? Are you such a friend for someone?

If so, thank him!

If not, ask him! With God nothing is impossible.

My Thoughts,
Prayers, Memories . . .

Use these pages to record your response to the thought starters
we've provided. You may want to write a poem, attach
a photo, or journal your ideas. However you choose
to respond, do so from a heart filled with
joy in our Lord's amazing grace.

Friendship is laughter.

Friendship is caring.

Friendship is encouragement.

Friends—Praying Together, Staying Together

Mary stayed with Elizabeth "about three months" (Luke 1:56). Despite the difference in their ages, the similarities in their circumstances brought them close. Their love and hope in the Lord did, too.

How did they spend those months? Scripture does not tell us, but based on Elizabeth's initial greeting and Mary's hymn of praise in response, we can guess they prayed together. They must have prayed a lot—for understanding, for courage, for wisdom, for faith.

If Elizabeth was "in her sixth month" (Luke 1:36) when Mary set out for Judea . . . well, you do the math. Together the women waited and then watched as the Lord fulfilled his promise to Zechariah through Gabriel. And if that promise proved true in baby John, then how could God fail to do what he had said to Mary through the angel?

Are you awaiting God's fulfillment of one or more promises he has made to you? Find a friend. Stay. Pray, until your Savior grants hope and peace.

*I've waited and watched my Lord
keep his word to me in these
times of need and challenge:*

1.

2.

3.

4.

5.

A friend who might value my encouragement in God's faithfulness for a challenge or need right now is_____.

One thing I could do for my friend is . . .

What a Friend!

If Mary had a camera, what photos might she have taken — and treasured — ever after? A very pregnant, laughing Elizabeth? The two of them eating dill pickle and roast lamb sandwiches? Might Elizabeth have snapped a photo of Mary, packing to return to the joys — and questions — that certainly awaited her?

The three months Mary and Elizabeth spent together surely changed them — forever. Friendship has a way of doing that. Even after we part, we carry friendships in our hearts forever. Still, saying goodbye is one of life's hardest passages.

In light of this, think about what a friend we have in Jesus! Knowing him has changed us forever. In him we receive God's gift of eternal life, certainly. What's more, his presence transforms even the bleakest trial. His presence brightens even the most radiant joy. He will never fail us or forsake us. (See Deuteronomy 31:6.)

Want a snapshot of his love? Christ on Calvary — arms outstretched — now *there's* a picture of grace!

What Friends!

My best friends have been . . .

The Lord Jesus has given me many times of laughter with my friends . . .

I have experienced these joys in my friendships . . .

Thanks, Lord, for . . .

What a Friend!

What a friend we
have in Jesus,
All our sins
and griefs to bear.
What a privilege to carry
Everything to God
in prayer!

Joseph Scriven 1865

Luke 2:51–52

Everyday Living

EMPOWERED BY GRACE

Almost everyone enjoys birthdays—the cake, ice cream, and confetti bring smiles to many faces. But most days aren't birthdays.

We take lots of photos at weddings. We want to remember the day forever. But most days aren't wedding days.

Christmas brings families together—often from all over the nation—as we celebrate and make memories to last a lifetime. But most days aren't Christmas.

Most days fill up with school, chores, jobs, bills, traffic, and alarm clocks. We settle for fast food instead of baked ham and sweet potatoes. We wash the car instead of watching the Super Bowl or World Series. In Luke 2:51–52, the holy writer summarizes those everyday days in Jesus' boyhood:

> *So he went back to Nazareth with them,*
> *and lived obediently with them.*
> *His mother held these things dearly, deep within herself.*
> *And Jesus matured, growing up in both body and spirit,*
> *blessed by both God and people.*
> THE MESSAGE

Had we followed the boy Jesus with a camera, would we have captured memorable moments, moments when beams of grace broke through to bathe the ordinary in the light of heaven's wonder and peace? No doubt! Mary "held these things dearly, deep within herself." Moments worth remembering!

But that was Jesus' life. Certainly we cannot expect God to flood our own lives with his grace in this way, day by day by ordinary day. Or can we? Scripture encourages us:

> *Stay with what you heard from*
> *   the beginning, the original message.*
> *Let it sink into your life.*
> *   If what you heard from the beginning*
> *   lives deeply in you, you will live*
> *   deeply in both Son and Father.*
> *This is exactly what Christ promised:*
> *   eternal life, real life!*
>
> 1 John 2:24–25 THE MESSAGE

Imagine it! Deep life. Real life. Eternal life. Memorable life. Everyday life—starting now!

How? By letting the good news of Jesus' unconditional acceptance, forgiveness, and love sink more and more deeply into your heart, abiding there, resting there, to make a real and eternal difference in your own life and, through you, in the lives of those around you.

Day by day. Every day!

My Thoughts,
Prayers, Memories . . .

Use these pages to record your response to the thought starters
we've provided. You may want to write a poem, attach
a photo, or journal your ideas. However you choose
to respond, do so from a heart filled with
joy in our Lord's amazing grace.

Everyday frustrations Jesus might reclaim for his glory . . .

Living deeply in both Son and Father
for me would mean . . .

Growing in Grace, Day by Day

Too soon old; too late wise. So goes a timeworn lament.

Most of us long for the benefits that wisdom brings. And we wish they came easily, in life's "Kodak moments," while we relax on the beach.

But like many things in life, growth in wisdom is a process. Even the Lord Jesus "increased"—grew—in wisdom (Luke 2:52 KJV).

Scripture tells us, "The fear of the LORD is the beginning of wisdom" (Proverbs 9:10 KJV). We don't *start* traveling wisdom's road until we recognize the Lord's authority over all of life, standing in awe of his majesty.

Yet even as we spot that on-ramp, we recognize we've already missed it. We have failed to obey. We have insisted on being our own authority, on setting our own standards.

This realization brings us to the next step on wisdom's road: a day-by-day recognition that in the face of our sin, God's mercy is available, always— and only—available through Christ.

Seeing my sin. Trusting my Savior.
As I think about these steps toward wisdom, I wonder . . .

Lord Jesus, I want to be truly wise.
Please . . .

Precious Moments

Watching Jesus grow up must have been amazing: Infant. Toddler. Child. Young man. The snapshots that could have been taken would have filled dozens of scrapbooks.

Mary treasured each moment, keeping them in a special place in her heart, wondering what it all could mean, trying to connect what the angels, shepherds, and Magi had told her. What was God up to?

Do you think about the day-by-day moments in your life in a similar way, treasuring even the "ordinary" moments of life as moments bearing the fingerprints of God? You can, you know. Consider his promise:

We know that in all things God works
for the good of those who love him,
who have been called according to his purpose.
Romans 8:28

In *all* things. Think about it! This makes even "ordinary" moments, holy moments.

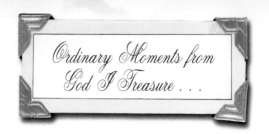

Ordinary Moments from God I Treasure . . .

Acts 18:24–28

For Every Generation

EMBRACED BY GRACE

Heart to Heart

Passion. Fervor. Zeal. Have you ever known anyone who taught or preached with a love for Jesus that went above and beyond the ordinary? Above and beyond expectations?

Apollos taught and preached like that. You and I both would have loved listening to him; Priscilla and Aquila did! But as they listened, they heard more than fervor. They heard niggling inaccuracies, statements that failed to live up to the complete truth about who Jesus is and what he has done for us.

Priscilla and Aquila could have arisen in holy zeal, correcting—and discrediting—Apollos in the public forum. Instead, Priscilla and Aquila took Apollos aside in kindness and concern.

They acknowledged his competence in the Scriptures (Acts 18:25). They remembered and respected the fact that Apollos had already "been instructed in the way of the Lord" (v. 25 ESV).

The result? More fully equipped, Apollos began to make short-term mission trips (v. 27). Eventually he joined the great apostle Paul's entourage (1 Corinthians 16:12). Apollos "greatly helped those who through grace had believed" (v. 27 ESV).

The Gospel continues to spread from heart to heart still today as God's people share the truths—and the love—of Christ with zeal and accuracy. Like a baton in a relay race, we pass the faith on. Individual by individual. Life by life. Heart by heart. The encouragement passes from generation to generation.

Someone has handed that baton off to you, to me. We get to pass it on to children, grandchildren, neighbors, friends, students, clients. As the Holy Spirit gave Apollos, Priscilla, and Aquila a sphere of influence, so he has given one to us.

We ask the Spirit for the zeal he worked in Apollos. We read and study Scripture with the goal of understanding the ways of God in Christ as accurately as possible. We approach others with the courtesy of Priscilla.

In your hearts regard Christ the Lord as holy, always being prepared to make a defense to anyone who asks you for a reason for the hope that is in you; yet do it with gentleness and respect, having a good conscience.

1 Peter 3:15–16 ESV

My Thoughts,
Prayers, Memories . . .

Use these pages to record your response to the thought starters
we've provided. You may want to write a poem, attach
a photo, or journal your ideas. However you choose
to respond, do so from a heart filled with
joy in our Lord's amazing grace.

Teachers, friends, and mentors who passed the
baton of faith to me . . .

Lord Jesus, help me pass the faith on to . . .

A lesson about my Lord's
love that I cherish . . .

Time Capsules

Imagine having been Billy Graham's Sunday school teacher. Or Mother Theresa's favorite aunt. Or the chief surgeon in the hospital where Joseph Lister began his career.

Giants in the church or the larger society may seem self-made, but no one springs fully mature onto the world's stage, ready to contribute. They, like the rest of us, need parents, teachers, mentors, role models. We cannot all serve as giants in our fields, but God does call all of us to influence others for good.

Priscilla and Aquila worked with Apollos. Their influence made an impact to the point that Apollos "greatly helped those who through grace had believed" (Acts 18:27 ESV). He went into a future they would never see and into places they would never go to share the mercy and forgiveness of Jesus. Apollos was a "time capsule" of sorts, to which Priscilla and Aquila had the honor of contributing.

Whose lives are you influencing?

As I consider opportunities to contribute to the careers, faith life, and future of others, I . . .

Dear Jesus,
Thank you for all those
> *gracious, grace-filled servants*
> *of yours who mentored me!*
> *Thanks especially for . . .*

I'm concerned for those
> *in whose lives you*
> *have placed me as*
> *a person of influence . . .*

Please help me . . .

Please help them . . .

In Service
to the Lord

Would you have walked into Apollos's life? He was eloquent.
He was evidently educated. He had at least some formal Bible
training, having been "instructed in the way of the Lord"
(Acts 18:25 ESV). He spoke and taught with fervor and
boldness (vv. 24, 26).

Many of us might have backed away from such an accomplished
and confident young man. "Let God work with him," we might
have told ourselves. "In time those rough edges will smooth off."

Not content with that, Priscilla and Aquila took the risk, took
the young man aside, and gently spoke the truth—in love—
in ways Apollos could receive and appreciate. They cared
enough—about Apollos, about Christ's church, and about
the truth—to address the gaps in Apollos's ministry.

Truth. Love. The balance is not easily managed as we invest
in the lives of those around us. God grant us the wisdom
of his Spirit to discern the ways we can best serve Jesus
by serving others in truth and love.

Passing On the Faith

Similarly, teach the older women to live in a way that is appropriate for someone serving the Lord. They must not go around speaking evil of others and must not be heavy drinkers. Instead, they should teach others what is good. These older women must train the younger women to love their husbands and their children, to live wisely and be pure, to take care of their homes, to do good, and to be submissive to their husbands. Then they will not bring shame on the word of God.

Titus 2:3–5 NLT

Someone who has modeled these verses for me is . . .

A better way I would like to do this is . . .

As I consider those whose lives have influenced me, both men and women, here are individuals for whom I thank God (list them here) :

I want to thank these people individually, as well as thanking God. Here's how I could do that (list ideas here) :

May my teaching drop as the rain, my speech distill as the dew, like gentle rain upon the tender grass, and like showers upon the herb. For I will proclaim the name of the LORD; ascribe greatness to our God!

Deuteronomy 32:2–3 ESV

If this book has made a difference in your life or if you have simply enjoyed it, we would like to hear from you. Your words will encourage us! You can reach us at:

Editorial Department
CTA, Inc., 1625 Larkin Williams Rd., Fenton, MO 63026-1205

or by e-mail at editor@CTAinc.com